Rx
Reading and Following the Directions for all Kinds of Medication

Carolyn Simpson
Penelope Hall, M.D.

THE ROSEN PUBLISHING GROUP, INC.

NEW YORK

Special thanks to pharmacist Tom Siegmann
for his valuable advice.

Published in 1994 by The Rosen Publishing Group, Inc.
29 East 21st Street, New York, NY 10010

First Edition

Manufactured in the United States of America.

Library of Congress Cataloging-in-Publication Data

Simpson, Carolyn.
    RX: reading and following directions for all kinds of medications /
Carolyn Simpson and Penelope Hall, M.D. — 1st ed.
        p.   cm. — (The Life skills library)
    Includes bibliographical references.
    ISBN 0-8239-1696-0
    1. Drugs—Administration—Juvenile literature. [1. Drugs. 2. Drugs,
Nonprescription.]   I. Title   II. Series.
RM147.S56 1994
615.5'8—dc20   94-702
                                                               CIP
                                                               AC

CONTENTS

DOCTORS:
GETTING THE MOST OUT
OF VISITS

My daughter, Michal, woke up one morning with a swollen face. We thought her allergies were acting up. One thing we knew for sure: She needed to see a doctor at once.

The doctor poked Michal's face and peered into her swollen eyes. "Well, she's allergic to something," he said.

"I just woke up this way," Michal told him.

"You haven't used different soap or bought a new perfume?"

"No, nothing's been different," she answered.

"Well, this may be one of those cases where we don't know the cause," the doctor said. "But I do know how to treat it. I'll order you some pills to take the swelling down, and we'll go from there."

Try to give your doctor complete and accurate medical information about yourself.

As Michal was walking out, she turned to the doctor and said, "Oh, by the way, I've got this funny bite mark on my leg. You don't think that has anything to do with my face, do you?"

Sure enough, that little mark over her knee turned out to be the bite of a fiddleback spider. When the doctor knew that, he ordered a whole different treatment. Had Michal not mentioned that one bit of information, she might not have recovered as quickly.

What's the point? Simple. When you consult a doctor, tell him or her everything. Don't leave out bits of information that you think are not important. Chances are, they may have a connection to your condition. Ever try putting together a puzzle with half the pieces missing?

When you consult a doctor, you both have jobs to do. The doctor gives a name to your problem, based on the information you provide. So, first of all, your job is to be totally honest. (This isn't the time to pretend that you never have headaches or lie awake at night. The doctor needs to know that.)

Probably the doctor will prescribe medication for you. Your second job is to make sure you understand when you're supposed to take it, how you're supposed to take it, and for how long. Sure, doctors tell you all that, but patients do not always listen the first time. It's okay to ask the doctor or the nurse to repeat the information. In fact, it shows you're concerned. Don't leave the office without knowing these four things:

1. When to take your medicine (the time of day).
2. How to take it (swallow, chew, insert it).
3. How long to take it (the number of days).
4. What side effects you might have.

If a doctor tells you that you might become constipated taking the medicine, and you don't know what constipated means, ask! Don't worry about seeming stupid. It's a lot more stupid to try to follow directions you don't understand.

If you're on a tight budget, you might ask the doctor for "samples" instead of a prescription. Very often, doctors have closets filled with sample medications that they can give you instead of prescribing the same thing. As expensive as medicines are these days, that's a big saving!

CHAPTER 2

NURSES:
HOW THEY CAN HELP YOU

Kara and Alicia sat in the girls' locker room. Alicia was lacing her sneakers, while Kara leaned against her locker with closed eyes.

"You don't think it's this infection that's making me feel so bad, do you?" Kara said.

"I thought you were taking something for it?" Alicia asked.

"I am taking something. Three times a day, as a matter of fact. But I itch all over."

"You worry too much. It's probably nerves. Have you got a test coming up or something?"

"I never got hives from worrying over a test before."

"What about the pills you're taking?" Alicia asked. "Are you allergic to them?"

Nurses are prepared to answer many of your questions about procedures and medications.

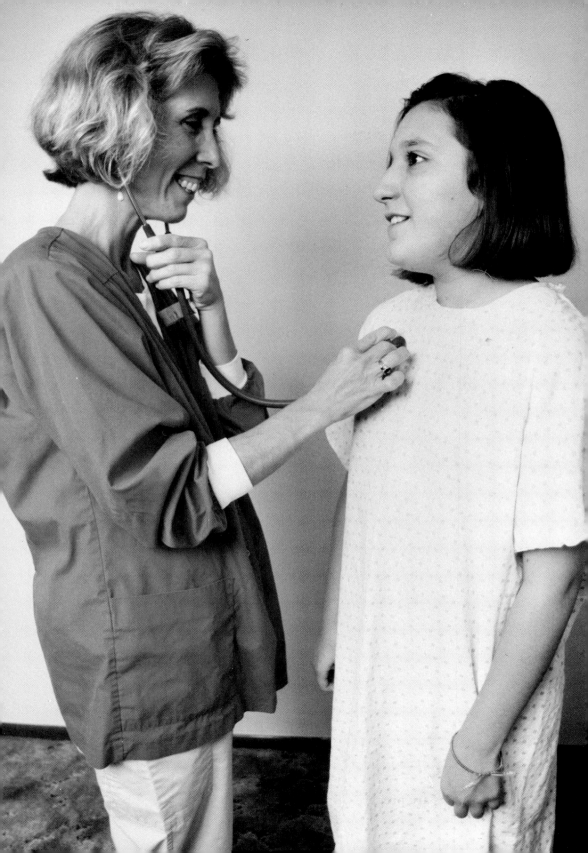

"Mom says I'm not allergic to anything," Kara said. "But I feel awful. And I can't breathe very well, either. It's like I can't get enough air."

"You should call your doctor," Alicia said, beginning to feel concerned.

"He's too busy, and besides, what would I say?"

"Well, at least, call the nurse. She could tell the doctor. In fact, maybe you should check with the school nurse first."

When Alicia dragged Kara to the infirmary, the nurse took one look at her and exclaimed, "What are you taking? You're having a reaction!"

Kara was one of the lucky ones; she recovered from her severe allergic reaction. "But why did you let yourself get so sick before you came to see me?" the nurse asked.

"I didn't know it was the medicine," Kara said.

"Even when you were having shortness of breath? That's one of the signs of an allergic reaction."

"Well, to tell you the truth, I didn't know what 'shortness of breath' meant," Kara said. "And I didn't want to bother anyone to find out. I didn't think it was important."

Remember, it is always important to know what to expect from the medicine you are given. Don't take chances. Get the facts clearly in your mind. If you get home from a doctor's appointment and still have questions, call the office back and ask for the nurse. You will probably discover that the nurse is more available than the doctor. And sometimes it's just plain easier to ask those embarrassing questions of a nurse.

Nurses are there to explain words you don't understand and to help you with many things. In this day and age, nurses do more than weigh you and take your blood pressure. It's just as much their job to answer your questions when they can, and to know when to relay information to the doctor.

Sometimes nurses know right off when you don't understand a term or procedure. But if they don't pick up on your confusion, its your job to ask.

CHAPTER

3

PHARMACISTS:
GETTING THEM TO HELP YOU

Nicholas had a problem.
He was constipated, or what his mother would call
"plugged up." The last thing he was going to do was
ask her for advice. He'd handle it himself. So he
drove over to the neighborhood drugstore. Actually, he
drove to the next town's neighborhood drugstore. He
didn't want anyone to recognize him.

He knew he needed a laxative. The TV commercials
told him that much. But which one? At the counter
he saw a whole row of products. Did he want a fiber
drink that was "all natural"? Did he want a pill?
Or would the laxative gum be more fun? And was a
laxative supposed to be fun, anyway?

Pharmacists can help customers choose the best product for
certain symptoms.

13

He picked up a package and squinted to read the label. A voice from behind him said, "Could I help you with something?"

He was ready to run out of the store when he turned and saw it was only the pharmacist. "I don't have a prescription," Nicholas said. "I just need something, um, from here." And he looked down at the row of laxatives.

"Maybe I could help," the man said.

"Do you know anything about laxatives?" Nicholas finally asked.

The pharmacist nodded. "I know enough to help you, I think," he said. "And if nothing else, I know when to tell you to see your doctor."

Pharmacists can do more than fill prescriptions. It's also their job to know about all those products you can buy without a prescription—the over-the-counter items. If you're wondering which product to buy, feel free to ask for help. The pharmacist should know what's good for bee stings or diarrhea, and can point out where the medicines are kept.

If you have a prescription to be filled, the pharmacist may suggest a generic brand. Generic brands are exactly the same as the name brands but less expensive. The only difference is in the name. Good pharmacists usually suggest generic brands to save you money.

The pharmacist also makes sense of those scribbles on your prescription. Your doctor may have written, "Take 1 tablet t.i.d." "Take 1 tablet three times a day." The pharmacist may further suggest that you take it right after meals, or in the morning, in mid-afternoon, and at bedtime. If you need to drink milk with the pills, he or she will tell you that, too. Any warnings or words of advice will be typed right onto the label. In some drugstores, the pharmacist attaches stickers to the label with warning information. Be sure to read these carefully.

The pharmacist should explain to you possible side effects. Ask, if you have any questions. He or she has probably heard about every side effect there is and knows which ones are serious and need reporting. He or she can even give you tips on swallowing pills if that gives you trouble.

Another good thing: These days the pharmacist usually stores information about customers on computer, so he or she will know if they're taking anything else that might be a problem with a new medicine. If your pharmacist knows you well, he or she may even remember what else you're taking. For this reason alone, you should buy all your medications at the same pharmacy.

Finally, be sure you know in the drugstore those four things you learned at the doctor's:

1. When to take your medication.
2. How to take it.
3. How long to take it.
4. What possible side effects exist.

INDICATIONS:

REASONS TO USE THE PRODUCT

"My gosh, Steven, you coughed all through math class. Are you taking something for it?"

Steven popped another cough drop in his mouth. "Just these," he said.

"Cough drops?" Sara exclaimed. You need something stronger. You're eating those things like candy."

"I'll run over to the pharmacy at lunch and find something," Steven said.

"Good idea," Sara said. "And don't just pick up the first thing you see."

At the pharmacy, Steven was surprised to find two whole shelves of cough remedies. Should he buy a liquid, a capsule—and what flavor?

Read all labels and packaging before taking any medication.

He grabbed a bottle of cherry-flavored expectorant and walked to the counter.

"I'll take this," he told the pharmacist. "And don't bother to put it in a bag. I've got this cough that won't go away."

The pharmacist looked at the bottle. "Well, you don't want an expectorant," he said.

"Why not? It says it's for coughs."

"Well, sometimes a person coughs because he needs to get stuff out of his throat. Then he needs an expectorant. An expectorant makes you cough.

"But," the pharmacist continued, "if you've just got a dry tickle in your throat, you need a cough suppressant. That will keep you from coughing."

"Now, how would I have known that?" Steven asked.

"It's right on the back of the bottle—under 'Indications'. Right there it tells you why you should use this product."

"Okay, then," Steven said. "Let me put this back and find what I really need."

In this section we're going to look at all the printing on the back and sides of bottles. Everything you need to know about using medication safely is included right there.

What is usually printed first on the back (or side) label is "Indications." That means "why you should use this product." If you're wondering what kind of medication to take for a headache, for example, you'd look at pain relievers that mention treating headaches under "Indications."

Of course, you need to know what symptoms you have, and then understand the words that describe them on the bottle or box. You'll already be tipped off as to what the medication does by looking at the front of the package. It briefly lists the symptoms it treats. Turn the package around to check out the indications for more specifics.

If you're not sure what a symptom means (for example, nasal congestion or heartburn), ask the pharmacist—not the store clerk. How are you supposed to know if you've got the symptoms described on the bottle, if you don't know what the words mean? Here is a list of some common symptoms and their meanings.

acid indigestion Your stomach aches or feels sour.

agitation Feeling restless, not able to sit still. Actually, this word usually applies to what might happen if you take too much of a medication.

constipation Inability to have a bowel movement (after several days' time), or passing small, hard pieces when you do.

gas A result of acid indigestion, having gas means feeling as if you need to burp. "Passing gas" is releasing gas from the rectum. Flatulence means the same thing.

heartburn Another word for acid indigestion, it is usually an ache or burning feeling mostly in your chest. (It does not mean heart attack.)

hemorrhoids Varicose veins that stick out of your

rectum. They may feel like large pimples, and they may itch or burn. They may also bleed.

insomnia Inability to fall asleep or stay asleep.

minor throat irritation A scratchy throat that you need to keep clearing.

nasal congestion Nasal refers to your nose, and congestion means to be stuffed up, having trouble breathing through the nose.

nausea Stomach upset; wanting to throw up (vomit).

neuralgia Nerve pain. It goes along with headaches and muscle pains.

sinusitis A sinus infection, usually with headache and a stuffy nose.

stool A bowel movement.

topical relief Relief of pain on the *outside* of your body, not *in* it.

To understand if a medication will work for you, start by doing two things. First, recognize your symptoms— decide in what way you are feeling bad. Second, look up those symptoms under "Indications" to see if the product treats them.

Even if it does treat your symptoms, however, the medication may still not be right for you. Read all information available to make yourself aware of any other things that might make the product dangerous to you.

There will be less chance of an overdose if you write down when and how much medication you take.

DIRECTIONS:
HOW TO USE THE PRODUCT

Cathy decided she had a *yeast infection. Her friend Megan took her to the pharmacy in their neighborhood and showed her the boxes of medications to treat vaginal yeast infections.*

After looking them over, Cathy chose a box and bought it.

"Now, tonight before you go to bed, fill the applicator with the cream. Put it in your vagina, like a tampon," Megan said. "It's no big deal. If I can do it, you can do it. It's a little messy, but you're going to bed afterward, so don't worry about it."

"How do I know how far up to push it?" Cathy asked, still sounding worried.

Always check to see that your prescription is correct. Your name and your doctor's name should appear on the label.

"Well, all I can say is you'll know by how it feels. But if you're that worried, I'll come over."

"Never mind, I'm just a little nervous," Cathy said. "Aren't there any directions?"

"If you're so stupid you need directions, look at the little folder that comes in the box. It has pictures telling you what to do. I'm telling you all you need to know, but if it makes you feel better, there are good directions."

Later that night, Cathy opened the box and took out the applicator. But instead of finding cream in a tube, she found tablets sealed in foil. She peeled one tablet out of the foil and looked at it. Well, surely a tablet goes in the mouth, she thought. Maybe they had a new version of this medication that Megan didn't know about.

She held up the tablet, preparing to swallow it. She thought it was awfully big. Just then, Megan's words came back to her. "If you're so stupid you need directions, look at the little folder that comes in the box."

Taking out the package insert, Cathy studied the picture. The woman in the illustration had put the tablet into the applicator and was inserting it into her vagina. These words jumped out at her: WARNING. FOR VAGINAL USE ONLY. Cathy read some more and felt relieved. Good thing I read the directions, she thought.

Directions are given for us to read. They tell us how we're supposed to use the product. And you certainly are not stupid for using them!

When you have chosen a product you think will treat your symptoms, read the next section, under "Directions." Here it will say whether you should take the product orally (by mouth), rectally (in the rectum), vaginally (in the vagina), or topically (on the surface of your skin or teeth). "For external use only" is another way of saying "Put this product on your skin only." If it is a pill or a liquid, the directions will suggest a dosage (often based on your age or weight) and tell you how often to take it. But just as important, the directions tell you how long to use the product; for example, "Use for three days only."

Sometimes you'll see the words, "Consult your physician" after an age group. This means that you should not take ANY dosage at all in this age group without getting an okay from your doctor.

Applying Drops

What the directions for eardrops or eyedrops may not tell you is exactly *how* to get the product where you want it to be. Vaginal suppositories and rectal suppositories have package inserts and diagrams; you can read them and follow the steps. But eardrops and eyedrops tell you: "Place one to two drops in the affected ear or eye." Now, that's easier said than done. Here are some tips to make the job easier:

Let's start with your ears. Lie down on your side, and have someone squeeze in a drop or two. Then lie still for a while so the medication will not run out. You can use a small bit of cotton, but it's best not to use anything. You don't want the cotton ball to absorb the medicine your ear needs.

The best way to use eyedrops is to lie on your back. Hold your eye open with one hand and have the bottle ready in your other hand. Count to three, then squeeze in a drop. Aim for the corner of your eye. If you blink before the drop goes in, wait a minute, then try again.

If you're still not sure how to use a product even after reading the directions, look around on the box for a number to call. Some products state, "If you have questions about this product, call us at _____" (an 800 number, which is a toll-free call). If there is no number given, ask your pharmacist for help. Never try to use a product without clearly understanding the directions.

WARNINGS AND SIDE EFFECTS

Buddy, a football player, came down with a terrible cough one season. He tried regular cough medicine, but it didn't help.

Buddy felt so weak that he couldn't even practice. The team doctor diagnosed his problem as bronchitis and prescribed an antibiotic. At first, some of Buddy's energy and appetite came back. But after a couple of days he felt worse in a different way. Now he couldn't lift his head off the pillow without feeling sick to his stomach.

Did he have some disease that the antibiotic couldn't treat? No. He simply had a common side effect of the antibiotic: nausea. The medication was making him sick, even though it was also killing the infection. The doctor simply prescribed an antinausea medication to take along with the antibiotic. He could have changed the antibiotic, but throwing away the whole *prescription would have been too expensive. Better just to order an inexpensive antinausea medicine.*

The moral of this story is to check ahead for possible side effects. It never occurred to Buddy that he was having a reaction to his medication.

Below the section called "Directions" on the package is another section worth reading, called "Warnings." This will tell you about any reasons why you should not be taking the product. A typical warning you may have read is: DO NOT TAKE THIS PRODUCT IF YOU ARE PREGNANT OR NURSING WITHOUT FIRST CONSULTING YOUR PHYSICIAN. All medications cross the placental boundary and affect the baby in your womb. You might need something, but the baby growing inside you doesn't. You might be warned not to "operate a vehicle or dangerous machinery while taking this medication." That means that this product is likely to make you drowsy or sleepy. You'll read here if you should take your pills with milk or food, or on an empty stomach. Most medications remind you to keep the product out of children's reach.

The warning section might also tell about the danger of mixing different medications. Sometimes two drugs taken together become twice as strong; sometimes they make each other useless. This warning may be listed under "Drug Interactions."

———

Know what to expect from your medication, and under what conditions you should or should not take it.

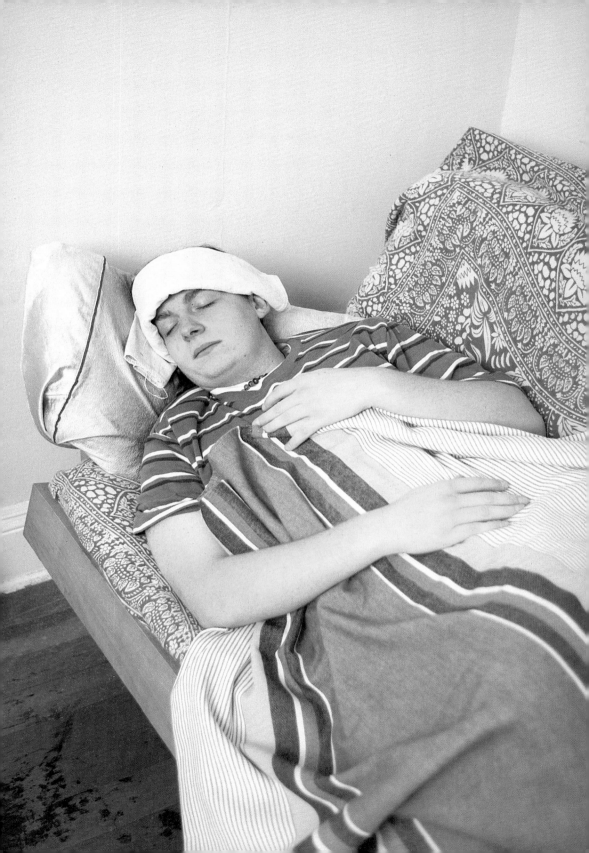

Contraindications

Contraindications is just another name for warnings. Here again, you'll be told reasons why you should not use the product. For example, if you already have high blood pressure, you wouldn't want to take any medication that would make the pressure even higher.

Usually, side effects of a medication are listed under "Warnings." But sometimes they're listed under a separate heading, "Adverse Reactions." The listing of side effects does not mean that you will get them all—just that you could get some of them. Side effects range from symptoms such as dry mouth to more severe symptoms such as shortness of breath. Be sure you know what all these terms mean. Shortness of breath, by the way, means difficulty in breathing, inability to get enough air. This is a dangerous sign. Call your doctor immediately, and STOP TAKING THE MEDICATION.

Adverse reactions are by definition bad. Some are more tolerable than others. Be alert for possible allergic reactions, which can be fatal. The first sign is usually a rash. Then you may develop hives (itchy, red spots), and finally shortness of breath. These symptoms tell you that your body is not handling the medication well.

Always check the ingredients of every product you use. They're also listed on the box or bottle. If you know you're allergic to something, see if it is used

in the making of the product. Allergic reactions
and adverse reactions are not simply side effects.
They are serious body responses. If you know
ahead of time what is normal to expect and what is
considered dangerous, you'll be quicker to realize
when you are in trouble.

PRESCRIPTION DRUGS

Alane left her doctor's office feeling worse than when she went in. She showed the written prescription to her friend, Tonya.

"Look at this. It's all in initials. How am I supposed to know how to take this stuff?"

"Let me see," Tonya said. Sure enough, the little white piece of paper didn't seem to be in English.

"It says Amoxil. I thought the doctor was giving me penicillin. And get this. He says, 'Take it Q.I.D.' Now what's that supposed to mean?"

Tonya frowned at the prescription. "Maybe the pharmacist can make sense out of it," she said.

Imagine the girls' surprise when the pharmacist typed up the label: *Take 1 tablet four times a day.*

Contact your pharmacy if you have any questions about your prescription.

The pharmacist then suggested the best times of day to take the medication and reminded Alane to take it for the full ten days. He also told her that Amoxil was a form of penicillin.

You really don't have to be able to read the doctor's writing. Most prescriptions look as if they are written in a foreign language. You should know what you are taking and why, but the pharmacist can do the translation for you.

Reading the label on your prescription medication is a different matter. There is important information on the label. At the top is your pharmacy's name and phone number. If you get home and have a question, you'll have the pharmacy's phone number right there on the bottle. You won't have to bother with the phone book.

Under that is usually the patient's name. Always check to be sure it is your name on the label. Pharmacists are human and can make mistakes. They may confuse your medication with the next person's. Don't take anything unless it has your name on it.

You'll also find the name of your medication (which may differ from what the doctor called it if the pharmacist is giving you the generic brand). Make sure you're taking what you're supposed to be taking. Then you'll find directions for taking the medication: one tablet, one teaspoon, or one applicatorful every three hours or twice a day, etc. Should you need to take the medication with food (or on an empty stomach), the pharmacist will either type this information on the label or attach a sticker. Even if you forget everything the pharmacist tells you, you should be able to check it all out by reading the label later.

You'll also find how many pills were prescribed. Count them to be sure you got the full amount. The date of your prescription is right there, too, as well as whether you can get refills. Some prescriptions you can refill without seeing the doctor again, but only if it says so on the prescription. If the doctor has written "prn" in the refill box, you can refill the prescription as often as you need.

A word of advice. If you've been taking certain pills for a while, and a new supply looks different, call the pharmacist. The doctor may have ordered a different dosage, so the pill is a different color. Or the drug manufacturer may change the color or shape of a medication. But mistakes can be made. Don't take something you're not sure about. If you have questions, call the pharmacist. He or she will welcome your concern.

BUYING, STORING, AND USING MEDICATION

If our world were a safer place, we wouldn't have to worry about people messing with our medicine before we even open it. But the truth is, we do have to worry. People have died from taking medicine that had been tampered with. But there are things you can do to be safe.

Check for Tampering

When you decide on a product, check to be sure the box is sealed. If it isn't, open the box and inspect the bottle. Does it have a plastic covering over the cap? If it has been broken, don't buy the bottle.

The proper dosage is as important as the proper medication.

37

Look for another. Don't buy any suspicious-look-ing product; that means with a torn wrapper or a cap not screwed on tightly.

If you buy capsules, look each capsule over care-fully before you swallow it. If one looks different from the rest, throw it away. Capsules are especially easy to open and then fit back together. Don't take chances.

Expiration Dates

Be sure not to take any medicine that is out of date. Check the expiration date on the back of the bottle or the end flap of the box. The date will either be written in ink or printed on the box. If you can't find a date, ask the pharmacist to help you. Every box must be dated. If the product is out of date, don't buy it. Also, check all the medications you have at home. If you find one with a past expiration date, throw that product away. Medicine loses its effectiveness (or can become stronger) when it's out of date.

Generic Brands

When you decide what type of product you need, you still have to choose among several brands. Is the brand you hear about on television better than the store's brand (often called the generic brand)? Generic brands are usually the same as the fancy brands; they just cost less. If you can find the generic brand, remember, it's just as good.

Problems of Storage

Always read the fine print. If the medicine is supposed to be stored in the refrigerator, it will say so.
If it is a prescription medication, the pharmacist will
tell you where to store it and will note it on the
label. If you store it in the refrigerator, be sure it's
away from kids (who might think it's a new drink).
If you think you might forget it's there, put it be-
side the milk or juice; then whenever you grab it
you'll remember the medicine.

   If your medication does not need to be stored in
the refrigerator (and don't put it there unless it says
so), keep it in a cool, dark place—for example, a
cupboard with doors that latch. If you have
younger brothers or sisters (or kids of your own),
put the medicine way up out of reach. Even hard-
to-open bottles should be out of kids' reach.

   Some medicine can lose its effectiveness if it is left
in the sun or in a warm room. Throw away medicine that starts to look "funny" (different from
when you first used it).

Opening Bottles

*Sallie woke up with a splitting headache. She found
the bottle of Tylenol in the medicine cabinet, but when
she tried to get the cap off, it wouldn't budge. Were
there directions for getting the cap off? All she could
find were arrows (one on the cap and one on the
bottle). I guess I'm supposed to line these two up, she
thought. After five tries, she finally pried the cap off.*

But she was no closer to getting the pills than before. Now she had to break through the foil seal. First, she tried to stick a fork into it, but it wouldn't fit. Then she pushed on the foil with her knuckle. It stretched some, but it didn't give way. Finally, she found the scissors and poked a hole in the seal. By now her head was throbbing.

She tore off the foil. To her dismay, she still couldn't get to the pills underneath. A huge wad of cotton blocked the way. She tried to cram her fingers into the bottle, but two wouldn't fit. She shook the bottle, hoping to knock some pills out. All they did was rattle around. Finally, she jammed the end of the fork into the bottle and pushed some of the cotton aside. Still, she couldn't reach a pill. Furious, she threw the bottle on the floor, and the pills spilled out all over the place.

You probably haven't had that much trouble getting a bottle of medicine open. But bottles with childproof caps are not easy to open. Sometimes you have to line up the arrows (the one on the cap to the one on the bottle) and then pull the cap off. Sometimes you have to push down on the bottle cap while twisting the bottle clockwise (and the cap counterclockwise). Both ways can be hard to do. So, if you don't have kids in your house, you might consider asking the pharmacist for regular caps.

By the way, there's an easy way to get the cotton wad out of the bottle: Use tweezers. You might

---

Always keep medicines safely out of the reach of young children.

want to keep a pair of tweezers in the medicine cabinet just for that purpose.

Pills may also come in sealed packets, and they can be tricky to open. Sometimes you'll spot right away where you're supposed to start peeling back the foil, but sometimes not. I've given up trying to find the right corner to peel back. I just take out the scissors and cut an opening very near the pill. That shortens the time spent tearing and bending, and the pill ends up undamaged.

Using Liquid Medicines

When the directions call for a ts. or t. of medicine, it means a teaspoon, but not the piece of silverware you use to stir your tea. It means a real measuring teaspoon. One T. or tbsp. means a tablespoon; again a real measuring tablespoon, not the kind in your silverware drawer.

You can also get a measuring cup at the pharmacy. The dosages are marked on the sides of the cup. Sometimes a cup comes with the medicine and fits right over the bottle cap.

If you use a dropper (with a baby, for example), remember to squeeze the end shut before putting it in the liquid. That way, when you release it, it sucks up enough medicine.

Swallowing Pills

Some people have a hard time swallowing pills. I used to have to chew aspirin because I couldn't get

it down any other way. You can imagine how the stuff tasted!

There's a trick to swallowing a pill. Put one under your tongue, and then take a big drink of water. If the pill doesn't slip down your throat with the first gulp, it will by the second. Keep drinking.

You can open a capsule by holding both ends and gently twisting in opposite directions. Stir the contents into applesauce or pudding. Of course, the medication will affect the taste of the food, but it's better than choking on a capsule.

Proper Dosage

Be careful about how much medicine you take. The fact that you have a really bad headache doesn't mean that four aspirin will be twice as good as two. When you take more pills than the directions recommend, you risk overdosing. Some medications build up in your bloodstream. What might not seem like an overdose may become one after steady abuse. Antihistamines can make you jumpy if you take them over too long a time. And if you take more than you should, you'll be too jittery to sleep at night.

Aspirin and acetaminophen can be deadly. "Take only as directed" means take only as many at a time as the directions say. If you can't correct your problem by taking the prescribed dosage on the bottle, you'll want to call your doctor, anyway. You have a bigger problem than you should be treating alone.

Don't take medicine any longer than specified. If it doesn't seem to be helping, tell your pharmacist that you are not getting any relief. He or she may recommend something else to use, or suggest that you call your doctor.

Shaking Liquid Medicines

Some medicine separates into layers when it sits around. If it says on the bottle to "shake vigorously," be sure to do that. Otherwise, you may not be getting the full benefit of the medicine.

What to Do in Case of Mistakes

If you've swallowed too many pills or taken something you shouldn't, call the Poison Control Center in your area. A statewide toll-free number is listed in your phone book. Look for it on the front inside cover or on the second or third page. It's a good idea to have the number handy before you ever need it. In a crisis, it's hard to calm down long enough to look up important numbers.

For similar reasons, write your pharmacy's number on the inside cover of your phone book. If you can't reach Poison Control, call your pharmacist.

Never assume that you should try to make yourself throw up. Sometimes that is the wrong thing to do. Always check with the Poison Control Center, your pharmacist, your doctor, or the emergency room of your local hospital.

GLOSSARY
EXPLAINING NEW WORDS

acetaminophen Medicine that relieves fever and pain without aspirin. Acetaminophen should be used instead of aspirin for children (anyone under 18) with chicken pox or the flu. Aspirin increases the risk of developing Reye's syndrome, a life-threatening illness.

b.i.d. Take two times a day (usually a.m. and p.m.).

contraindication A reason why you should not take a particular product.

expectorant Ingredient in cough medications that causes you to cough to get rid of phlegm in your throat and lungs.

expiration date The date when the medicine is no longer effective.

generic brand General class of medications that are the same as the name brands but cost less.

h.s. Take at bedtime (hour of sleep).

orally To be taken by mouth.

prn Take as you feel the need.

q. Shorthand for "every." "Take prn q. 4 hrs." means "Take every 4 hours if you need it."

q.i.d. Take four times a day.

rectally To be inserted into the rectum.

t.i.d. Take three times a day.

topical Same as "for external use only." Use the product only on your skin or on your tooth.

vaginally To be inserted into the vagina.

x. Shorthand for "times." For example, "Take three doses" might be written, "Take 3x."

FOR FURTHER READING

Arnold, Caroline. *Pain. What Is It? How Do We Deal with It?* New York: William Morrow & Co., Inc., 1986.

Clayman, Charles B., Kunz, Jeffrey R.M., and Meyer, Harriet S. *The American Medical Association Home Medical Adviser.* New York: Random House, 1988.

Edelson, Edward. *The ABCs of Prescription Drugs.* Garden City, NY: Doubleday and Co., Inc., 1987.

Funk and Wagnalls Family Medical Guide. Funk and Wagnalls Corporation, 1993 edition.

LeMaster, Leslie Jean. *Bacteria and Viruses.* Chicago: Childrens Press, 1985.

PDR Family Guide to Prescription Drugs. Montvale, N.J.: Medical Economics Data, Inc., 1993.

Tanner, Ogden. *The Prudent Use of Medicines.* Alexandria, VA: Time-Life Books, 1981.

Watterson, Kathryn. *The Safe Medicine Book.* New York: Ballantine Books, 1988.

INDEX

A
adverse reactions, 30–31
allergic reactions, 5–6, 10,
    30–31
Amoxil (*see* penicillin)
asking consumer questions,
    6, 10–11, 14–15, 35
    (*see also* toll-free call)

C
childproof caps, 40
contraindications (*see* warning)

D
directions (for use of product),
    23–26, 34, 43
doctor, consulting a, 6, 25, 44
drug interactions, 28

E
expectorant, 18
expiration date (on medication),
    38

G
generic brands, 14, 34, 38

I
indications, definition of, 18

L
laxative, 13

M
medication
    liquid, 42, 44
    overdose of, 43–44
    samples of, 7
    storage of, 28, 39
    taking, 42–44
    what to know about, 6–7, 15

N
nurse, talking to the, 11

P
penicillin, 33–34
pharmacist, 13–15, 18, 33, 34,
    35, 38, 39, 40, 44
placental boundary, 28
Poison Control Center, 44
prescription drugs, 33–35

47

About the Authors

Carolyn Simpson teaches psychology and communication classes at
Tulsa Junior College, Tulsa, Oklahoma. She has worked as a clinical
social worker in both inpatient and outpatient settings.

Penelope Hall, M.D., is a board-certified internist, practicing in
Billerica, Massachusetts. Both she and Ms. Simpson grew up in
Augusta, Maine. They collaborated on another book: *Careers in
Medicine*, as well as a science project back in eighth grade.

Photo Credits

All photos on cover and in book by Mary Lauzon.

Design & Production by Blackbirch Graphics, Inc.